Tales from the Troubled South

Civil Rights in Alabama

Catherine McGrew Jaime

Other Books by Catherine Jaime:

The Rocky Road to Civil Rights in the United States

Da Vinci: His Life and His Legacy

Leonardo the Florentine

York Proceeded On: The Lewis and Clark Expedition Through The Eyes of Their Forgotten Member

Creative Learning Connection
8006 Old Madison Pike, Ste 11-A
Madison, AL 35758
www.CreativeLearningConnection.com

Table of Contents

Introduction

In Martin Luther King Jr.'s final speech in 1968 he spoke of a "mental flight" from Egypt up through the time of Martin Luther and on forward to his own time.

Reverend Martin Luther King, Jr.

In this little book, I want to take a mental flight backwards to the beginning of the Civil Rights struggle in Alabama. We will have to go back before the march from Selma to Montgomery, back further than the church bombings in Birmingham, back before Rosa Parks' refusal to give up her seat on the bus.

Rosa Park's Congressional Medal of Honor

We will have to take our mental flight back to at least the end of the nineteenth century. There, only a few decades after the end of the Civil War, in the little Alabama town of Tuskegee, we can find some of what I consider to be the beginnings of the Civil Rights movement in Alabama.

An Early Class at Tuskegee

Civil Rights, the desire shared by all to be given the most basic of human rights, has had a long and painful struggle in the United States. Much of that struggle took place within the borders of Alabama.

But I have been saddened by the number of students **and** adults I've met in Alabama who've never heard most of these important stories.

So, I've attempted to gather them here, in one easy to read place, for those in Alabama who need a bit of a timeline to know their history better; but also for those outside of Alabama who would like to know more about Civil Rights and don't know where to begin.

If you want an overview of the road to Civil Rights, you might enjoy *the Rocky Road to Civil Rights in the United States*. This annotated timeline will give you many more dates and names to get you started in a general study of Civil Rights.

This book is not an encyclopedic look at this important topic, but merely an introduction that I hope will help many see how long the struggle has really lasted; and how much so many gave in the fight.

Before we get to the first of many steps in the road to Civil Rights in Alabama, we'll go back almost two hundred years further to when slavery first came to Alabama, and briefly mention two famous slaves (Dred Scott and Sojourner Truth) who crossed through Alabama (literally for one and figuratively for the other).

*Reverend King Statue
in Birmingham*

SLAVERY IN ALABAMA

In 1721, almost one hundred years before Alabama became a state, the first slaves were brought to Mobile.

Over time the percentage of enslaved people in Alabama jumped to thirty percent and by the end of the Civil War over forty-five percent of the state's total population were slaves. Many of them were bought and sold in the slave auction houses in Mobile and Montgomery.

Slave Auction

DRED SCOTT

In 1818, Dred Scott was brought from Virginia to Northern Alabama with his master's family. He remained in Alabama for twelve years (Huntsville and Florence) before moving on to St. Louis, Missouri. (In fact his first wife and one of his children are both buried in a small slave cemetery in Huntsville.)

In Missouri Scott was sold to a U.S. Army surgeon who took Scott to Illinois, the Wisconsin Territory, and then back to Missouri. In

1846, after the doctor's death, Scott sued for his freedom in the Missouri courts, on the grounds that he had lived in a free territory. A Missouri jury actually decided that Scott and his wife should be freed, but the case was appealed by the owner's widow.

Dred Scott

After being heard in a federal court, the Supreme Court finally heard the case in 1856, when it ruled against Scott. Chief Justice Roger Taney's majority opinion argued that as a black man and as a slave Scott was not a citizen of the United States. Taney also wrote that black men *"had no rights which the white man was bound to respect."*

Chief Justice Taney

While the Court ruled against him in one of the Supreme Court's most infamous decisions, Scott did eventually receive freedom from his third master, the son of his original master, who had become an abolitionist.

Sojourner Truth

In 1799 New York started a gradual, twenty-eight year process of emancipating its slaves. Sojourner Truth was promised her freedom a year earlier than the law required, but then her master backed out of his agreement.

After doing sufficiently more work than he had required of her, Sojourner Truth ran away with her infant daughter. Actually, in her words, *"I did not run off, for I thought that wicked, but I walked off, believing that to be all right."*

Sojourner Truth

Soon after escaping to freedom she learned that her old master had sold her five-year-old son to a new owner in Alabama, violating New York laws against the selling of a minor slave child across state lines.

Sojourner put all her energies into a court battle. Winning the return of her son, Sojourner Truth became the first black woman in the United States to sue a white man and win.

TUSKEGEE INSTITUTE

In the post-Civil War South, thousands of ex-slaves suddenly found themselves in need of becoming self-sufficient.

In the years that followed, two very different men, Lewis Adams, a former slave, and George W. Campbell, a former slave owner, dreamed of opening a "normal school" for blacks in Alabama.[1] In 1881, their

---

[1] *Normal schools were the first teachers' colleges in the country, training high school graduates in the teaching*

dream was realized with the opening of the Tuskegee Institute.

Dr. Booker T. Washington

Dr. Booker T. Washington, also a former slave, was hired as the first president of Tuskegee. One of the first things he did was to purchase the land of a former plantation on which to build the school.

---

standards or "norms" of teaching.

Washington was dedicated to the pursuit of self-reliance and he focused much of his efforts at the teachers' school on teaching practical skills, such as farming, brick-making, cabinetmaking, carpentry, printing, and shoemaking.

Dr. Washington's Home

In 1895, Washington spoke at the Cotton States and International Exposition in Atlanta. His speech was well received by most Southern whites, but not so well received by some blacks.

Washington spoke out: *"To those of my race who depend on bettering their condition in a foreign land or who underestimate the importance of cultivating*

friendly relations with the Southern white man, who is their next-door neighbor, I would say: 'Cast down your bucket where you are' – cast it down in making friends in every manly way of the people of all races by whom we are surrounded. Cast it down in agriculture, mechanics, in commerce, in domestic service, and in the professions."

He continued on, *"In all things that are purely social, we can be as separate as the fingers, yet one as the hand in all things essential to mutual prog-ress...The wisest among my race understand that the agitation of questions of social equality is the extremist folly..."*

That was not the direction that many blacks in the post-Civil War world wanted to go.

An important thing that Dr. Washington did at Tuskegee was to convince George Washington Carver, also a former slave, to come south to Tuskegee as a professor in 1896.

Over the next forty-six years, Carver taught agriculture in and out of Tuskegee, making a major contribution to improving agricultural methods in the South, helping Southern blacks **and** whites in the process.

Professor George Washington Carver

In 1946 Dr. Booker T. Washington became the first black to be honored on a U.S. coin.

Jim Crow Laws

Jim Crow laws throughout the South limited the civil rights of blacks through mandatory segregation in public transportation, schools, restaurants and more.

In many places the laws were on the books for almost one hundred years. In some places, including Mobile, curfews for blacks were included in the Jim Crow laws.

1904 Caricature
of Jim Crow's
"Separate But Equal"

"SCOTTSBORO BOYS"

During the Great Depression, nine black teenagers riding the rails were removed from a train in Scottsboro, and then falsely accused of raping two white women.

Eight of the nine were originally sentenced to death by all-white juries; only the twelve-year-old did not receive a death penalty.

After numerous mistrials and appeals, the sentences were upheld by the Alabama Supreme Court and then overturned by the U.S. Supreme Court.

Even then, the young men remained in jail. In 1937 the charges against five were finally dropped. Three of the others were eventually paroled in 1938, 1944, and 1948.

The last young man escaped jail in 1948. (In 1976, Governor George Wallace pardoned all nine of the "Scottsboro Boys," though only one lived long enough to receive the pardon.)

TUSKEGEE AIRMEN

When the "Tuskegee Experiment" was started in Tuskegee to train black airmen, funding and support was a problem until the first lady, Eleanor Roosevelt, intervened.

First Lady Eleanor Roosevelt

In July 1941, the first class of black airmen started

training in Tuskegee, Alabama. Of the thirteen who started, five successfully completed the training.

Tuskegee Airmen

Over the next five years, 996 pilots graduated from the training at Tuskegee. Four hundred and fifty of those pilots served overseas in the 99th Pursuit Squadron/99th Fighter Squadron or the 332nd

Fighter Group. The 332nd Fighter Group pilots painted their aircraft tails red to distinguish themselves from the other fighters.

Tuskegee Airmen in Ramitelli, Italy

In 1943 the 99th Fighter Squadron deployed to French Morocco. Within three months, Lt. Charles Hall had scored the squadron's first strike, the first black fighter pilot in the U.S. Armed Forces to shoot down an enemy aircraft.

Even with their early successes, there were many in the United States fighting to keep the 99th Fighter Squadron out of combat. Their commander, Colonel Davis, had to appear before the War Department's Advisory Committee on Negro Troop Policies to convince them to let his squadron continue in combat.

Eventually, the Squadron was moved to combat support in Italy. Within a few months, black fighter pilots had proved their worth in the air defense of Anzio.

Tuskegee Airman Edward M. Thomas, March 1945.[2]

---

[2] Photographed by Toni Frissell

During the war, Tuskegee Airmen shot down over two hundred enemy aircraft, while never losing one of the planes they were escorting. By the time the war was over, Tuskegee Airmen had received over 800 medals, and proved beyond a shadow of a doubt that black pilots were fully capable of serving in combat.

BROWN V. BOARD OF EDUCATION

In 1954, the United States Supreme Court banned school discrimination in their unanimous *Brown versus Board of Education* decision. The Supreme Court ordered lower courts to use "all deliberate speed" in desegregating schools.

In response, 1,200 white businessmen met in Selma, organizing the White Citizens Council to protest school desegregation. The Alabama Board of Education voted to maintain school segregation, and developed "pupil placement laws" that claimed to place students in school on the basis of other standards, rather than race, as a way of keeping the segregation status quo.

Rosa Parks
& the Montgomery Bus
Boycott

After hearing of the Brown decision against segregated schools, talk began in Montgomery of a boycott of the city's segregated buses. In the spring of 1955 a fifteen-year-old black girl, Claudette Colvin, was arrested for refusing to give up her seat on a Montgomery city bus.

There was talk of a boycott of the city buses at the time, but the decision was made to wait. The brutal murder of a young black boy from Chicago in Mississippi that August further angered the black community.

The Women's Political Council, along with their president, Professor Jo Ann Robinson, helped make plans for a boycott in the near future.

In December, the right circumstances finally came together for the boycott. Returning home from work one Thursday evening, Mrs. Parks sat in the front of the "blacks only" section of the back of the bus, directly behind the "whites only" section.

When another white passenger boarded the bus, all four black passengers in the next row (including Mrs. Parks) were required by law to give up their seats and stand. Mrs. Parks refused, even after being ordered to stand by the bus driver.

When she wouldn't budge, the driver called the police and Mrs. Parks was promptly arrested. (Mrs.

Parks would be asked later if she had kept her seat because she was tired: *"No, the only tired I was, was tired of giving in."*)

The Bus Mrs. Parks was riding (The Bus is now at the Henry Ford Museum in Michigan)

As a member of the NAACP (National Association for the Advancement of Colored People) and a prominent member of the black community, the forty-two-year-old Mrs. Parks was a good foundation on which to build a bus boycott.

*Rosa Parks
(Dr. King in the
background)*

When E.D. Nixon, an early Civil Rights Activist in Montgomery, heard of her arrest, he posted bail for her, and asked her permission to use her arrest as the excuse for a bus boycott in Montgomery.

Miss Jo Ann Robinson, president of the Women's Political Council, helped organize a one-day boycott of the city buses for the next Monday, passing out thousands of mimeographed handouts throughout the weekend.

On Friday evening, Reverend L. Roy Bennett chaired a meeting of civil rights leaders and ministers at his church, the Mount Zion AME Zion Church, to discuss the boycott. It was agreed that the ministers would help spread the word of the boycott in their churches on Sunday. Dr.

Martin Luther King, Jr., pastor of Dexter Avenue Baptist Church, hoped they would get at least sixty percent cooperation in the boycott. But when the day of the boycott came, almost every city bus was without a black rider onboard.

Dr. Martin Luther King, Jr.

King wrote of the day, *"A miracle had taken place, the once dormant and quiescent Negro community was now fully awake."*

Monday afternoon the group of organizers met at Mount Zion AME Zion Church again, where they formed the Montgomery Improvement Association and elected King as president.

Then the discussion ensued as to whether to continue the boycott beyond one day. Mr. Nixon spoke out in anger at the meeting, *"What's the matter with you people? ...The time has come when you men are going to have to learn to be grown men or scared boys.*"

That evening a mass meeting was held at Holt Street Baptist Church. It started with the singing of the hymn, *Onward Christian Soldiers* and ended with *My Country Tis of Thee*.

During the evening, Martin Luther King, Jr. gave his first civil rights' speech, "*If we are wrong, the Constitution of the United States is wrong. If we are wrong, God Almighty is wrong."*

When the vote was taken among those who had come to the meeting, the decision was unanimous that the boycott should continue.

The boycott would last 381 days, and would be referred

to as a *"Negro Revolt."* For more than a year, through cold weather and hot weather, black citizens of Montgomery walked, put together car pools, and formed their own private taxi services.

Across the country, black churches purchased shoes to send to Montgomery to replace the ones being worn out by the walkers.

Sister Pollard, seventy-years-old during the bus

boycott, explained, *"My feet is tired, but my soul is rested."*

The local white response to the boycott was strong. When legal pressure didn't put an end to the boycott, they resorted to violence.

Less than two months into the boycott, Dr. King's home was bombed. When a crowd of concerned citizens gathered around the home, King addressed them, *"Remember, if I am stopped, this movement will not stop, because God is with the movement."*

Fred Gray, one of only two black attorneys in Montgomery, filed a lawsuit challenging the bus segregation law. Several months later a Federal District Court ruled bus segregation unconstitutional, but the city appealed it to the Supreme Court.

Boycotters were often attacked and protestors were often arrested. But the boycott continued. After more than a year of boycotts, the Montgomery bus line had lost more than fifty percent of its income.

Just over one year after the bus boycott had begun, the city ordinance was finally declared unconstitutional by the U.S. Supreme Court. Dr. King and Rev. Glen Smiley, a white minister, celebrated by riding in the front seat of a bus together.

A sad footnote to the Bus Boycott: Soon after the boycott ended, the Parks family moved to Detroit because of the continued death threats they were receiving.

SOUTHERN MANIFESTO

In response to recent Supreme Court decisions banning segregation, seventy-seven Southern Representatives and nine-teen Senators came together to express their displeasure in the *Southern Manifesto*. They represen-ted eleven states, including Alabama:

"...The unwarranted decision of the Supreme Court in the public school cases is now bearing the fruit always produced when men substitute naked power for established law."

"...We regard the decisions of the Supreme Court in the school cases as a clear abuse of judicial power."

"...This unwarranted exercise of power by the Court, contrary to the Constitution, is creating chaos and confusion in the States principally affected. It is destroying the amicable relations between the white and Negro races that have been created through ninety years of patient effort by the good people of both races."

"It has planted hatred and suspicion where there has been heretofore friendship and under-standing…"

"You have to be prepared to die before you can begin to live."

~Rev Fred Shuttlesworth

REVEREND FRED SHUTTLESWORTH "BOMBINGHAM"

In 1956, when the NAACP refused to turn over a list of its members to the state of Alabama, the state banned the organization within the state. (Two years later the U.S. Supreme Court would overturn the state's decision, siding with the NAACP on the grounds of freedom of speech and freedom of association.)

In response to the ban, Reverend Fred Shuttlesworth met with six other ministers and helped organize the Alabama Christian Movement for Human Rights (ACMHR). Shuttlesworth was the first president of the new organization. *"They can outlaw an organization, but they can't outlaw the movement of a people determined to be free."*

Reverend Shuttlesworth Statue in Birmingham

When the Supreme Court ruled that the bus segregation in Montgomery was illegal, Shuttlesworth announced that ACMHR would test segregation in Birmingham.

In a Christmas Day sermon that year, Shuttlesworth said, *"If it takes being killed to get integration, I'll do just that thing. For God is with me all the way."*

Members of the local KKK were willing to do just that, bombing his home and church later that night. The mattress Shuttlesworth had been sleeping on was even destroyed.

When Shuttlesworth spoke to the concerned crowd assembling after the bombing, he assured them, *"The bomb had my name on it, but God erased it."*

Two weeks later, four black churches and two homes were bombed…Over the next eighteen years, more than fifty bombs would be set off in Birmingham, targeting those in the Civil Rights Movement, and earning the city the tragic nickname *"Bombingham."*

When Shuttlesworth heard of the Supreme Court's decision that schools must be desegregated, he remarked, *"I felt like I was a man, like I had rights."* In response to the deseg-regation orders, Rev. Shuttlesworth tried to enroll his daughters at an all-white school, and was beaten by police.

Shuttlesworth assisted Dr. King and Rev. Abernathy in forming the Southern Christian Leadership Conference (SCLC), and continued in his pursuit of civil rights in and out of Birmingham for many years.

Reverend Ralph Abernathy

Reverend Shuttlesworth spoke of his numerous arrests for the cause of civil rights, *"I was in jail so many times I quit counting after twenty."*

Even though Shuttlesworth moved his family to Cincinnati, Ohio in 1961 to protect them, a CBS documentary on Birmingham that year called Shuttlesworth *"the man most feared by Southern racists."*

FREEDOM RIDES

Segregation on interstate buses and trains had been an issue in the United States for many, many years.

In 1946, in *Morgan v. Virginia*, the Supreme Court had ruled segregation in interstate travel to be unconstitutional and that year sixteen men had tested the ruling with a *Journey of Reconciliation* through the Upper South. Many of the riders were arrested during their two week trip.

The Interstate Commerce Commission again banned segregated interstate travel laws in 1955. And in 1960 (in *Boynton versus Virginia*) the Supreme Court declared segregation on interstate transportation to be unconstitutional once again.

In 1961 Reverend Shuttlesworth assisted CORE (Congress on Racial Equality) in organizing Freedom Rides to test the ruling, modeled after the 1947 ride.

Volunteer riders were required by CORE to sign a waiver intended to let them know the dangers they might be facing:

"I understand that I shall be participating in a nonviolent protest against racial discrimination, that arrest or personal injury to me might result..."

Freedom Rides began in Washington D.C. and were destined for New Orleans. Several hundred black and white "Freedom Riders" participated over the summer, placing black and white riders in adjoining seats and black riders in front seats.

The first thirteen riders (seven black and six white) made it through Virginia and North Carolina without too much difficulty, but trouble began when they crossed into South Carolina. Birmingham Sherriff "Bull" Connor helped plan an attack on the first bus to cross into Alabama.

Its tires were slashed by a mob, who then followed the

bus in their cars until it was forced to stop. At that point the bus was attacked with firebombs. Riders escaping the burning bus were beat by the attackers, who were eventually scared off by highway patrolmen.

Injured riders were taken to a local hospital, where they were still in danger. Reverend Shuttlesworth organized private cars to pick up the injured riders in the middle of the night to carry them to safety.

The second bus had arrived in Anniston an hour behind the first. Klansmen boarded the bus and beat the riders severely. When the bus arrived in Birmingham the riders were attacked again with the assistance of the police under Bull Connor.

When the U.S. Attorney General Robert Kennedy heard of the violence in Alabama, he sent an assistant to try to calm the situation. Kennedy wanted the rides to stop, for the safety of all involved, but Civil Rights leaders did not want the violent measures against them to win out and pressed to continue.

Robert Kennedy

Replacement riders were brought in. Another bus was escorted to the Montgomery city limits, where the highway patrolmen deserted their posts, allowing another set of riders to be attacked and beaten.

Just over two weeks into the rides, more than 1500 people met in Rev. Abernathy's church in Montgomery to honor the Freedom Riders. A mob of more than 3,000 whites surrounded the church, threatening those on the inside, including Dr. King and Rev. Shuttlesworth.

Attorney General Robert Kennedy called in federal marshals to stop the violence. Governor Patterson then brought in the Alabama National Guard to settle things down.

The next day more riders came in to replace the injured riders. The Alabama and Mississippi governors then agreed to protect the riders from further violence, in exchange for the Federal Government backing out.

The bus left Montgomery and made it safely to Jackson, Mississippi, where the riders were all promptly arrested for violating local segregation laws.

The rides continued for the next four months, through the summer. More than 450 riders participated, and more than 300 were arrested in Jackson alone. Many of the riders followed up their rides with attempts to desegregate waiting rooms, restaurants, and more.

Robert Kennedy was quoted as saying that he did *"not feel that the Department of Justice can side with one group or the other in disputes over Constitutional rights."*

But that fall the Kennedy Administration pressured the Interstate Commerce Commission to issue new regulations against segregation in bus and train terminals.

PROJECT C – CONFRONTATION

In 1963, Reverend Shuttlesworth convinced Martin Luther King, Jr. to come to Birmingham to lead sit-ins and marches to protest segregation (Project C – Confrontation).

Dr. King was arrested on Good Friday for his participation in the protests and put in solitary confinement. While there he read a statement in the *Birmingham Times* by local white ministers referring to him as a troublemaker, and calling the protests *"unwise and untimely."*

In response King wrote his famous *"Letter from a Birmingham Jail"* where he chastised the ministers, *"For years now I have heard the word 'Wait!' It rings in the ear of every Negro with a piercing familiarity. This 'wait' has almost always meant 'never.'"*

King's release from jail was followed by plans for "D Day." Civil Rights Leader

James Bevel explained the rationale behind the day:

"Most adults have bills to pay...But the young people... are not hooked with all those responsibilities. A boy from high school has the same effect in terms of being in jail, in terms of putting pressure on the city, as his father, and yet there's no economic threat to the family, because the father is still on the job."

So, on May 2, more than fifty children between six and eighteen gathered in front of Sixteenth Street Baptist Church, heading downtown.

As they headed through the Kelly Ingram Park singing *"We Shall Overcome,"* they were all arrested, but they were followed by another group of kids, and another, and another, until over 900 children had been arrested.

The next day over 1,000 schoolchildren gathered at the Park. With no more room in his jails, Bull

Connor brought out fire hoses and police dogs to attack the children, rather than let them continue their march downtown.

Pictures of the attacks made the nightly news all over the country, enraging many who had been ignoring the civil rights violations previously.

President Kennedy reacted to the attacks with uncharacteristic sympathy, *"I can understand why the Negroes of Birmingham are tired of being patient."*

In hopes of bringing the demonstrations to an end, businesses in downtown Birmingham were soon agreeing to integration demands.

SIXTEENTH STREET BAPTIST CHURCH

As things heated up in Birmingham, Sixteenth Street Baptist Church was used often for mass meetings and as a rallying point for protestors, including for the marches from Project C.

The Reverends Bevel, Shuttlesworth, and King were frequent speakers at the church.

Reverend James Bevel

Four months after the "Project C" and "D Day" marches, the Sixteenth Street Baptist Church in Birmingham was bombed with nineteen sticks of dynamite.

Four young black girls preparing for "Youth Sunday" were killed by the explosion, again bringing a national outcry. The FBI investigated the case, identifying four suspects, but soon dropped the case, claiming civil rights activists had bombed the church themselves.

It would be almost forty years before charges were finally brought against the four KKK members responsible.

GOVERNOR GEORGE WALLACE

In 1963 George Wallace ran for Alabama governor on the promise of *"segregation now, segregation tomorrow, segregation forever."*

Governor George Wallace

His policy was quickly put to the test when two black students enrolled at the

University of Alabama. Governor Wallace, acting as University registrar, blocked the students from entering the school to register.

President Kennedy called out the Alabama National Guard, who ordered Wallace out of the way so the students could enter to register.

Twenty years later, Wallace won his fourth term as governor of Alabama, this time running on a platform of racial and religious tolerance.

SELMA TO MONTGOMERY MARCH

In Dallas County only one to two percent of eligible black citizens had successfully registered to vote in more than ten years of attempts. SNCC (Student Nonviolent Coordinating Committee) workers arrived in Selma in 1963 to begin pushing to get more blacks registered.

In spite of beatings, threats, and arrests, the workers continued their efforts. When thirty-two black teachers attempted to register, they were promptly fired by the white school board.

A year into their efforts, a local judge issued an injunction against three or more people gathering to even discuss civil rights. The injunction suppressed civil rights activities in the area for six months.

But on January 2, 1965 Dr. King arrived in Selma from Atlanta and addressed a mass meeting of 700 in Brown Chapel, defying the injunction, and kicking off the "Alabama Project" – designed to help bring the vote to the disenfranchised black community:

"Today marks the beginning of a determined, organized, mobilized campaign to get the right to vote everywhere in Alabama."

Voter registration efforts increased after the meeting in Dallas County and surrounding counties. Two weeks later, January 18, was declared as "Freedom Day," a day to focus on voter registration efforts in Dallas County and surrounding counties. Martin Luther King, Jr. was arrested on that date, and again on February 1.

After Dr. King's arrest, Malcolm X came and spoke in Selma. He made it clear that he did not support King's non-violent measures, not believing they would succeed. (Less than three weeks later Malcolm X was shot and killed in New York City.)

Malcolm X

How much people in the Marion/Selma area were

moved by Malcolm X's methods versus Martin Luther King's methods is unclear. But within a month, violence had come to the Selma area, one way or another.

On February 18 an evening march of 400 - 500 people was planned from the Zion Methodist Church in Marion to the local jail where SCLC field secretary James Orange was being held.

Here is where the details of what happened that night begin to deviate. One version of the story is that the marchers were peaceful as they left the church, planning to sing hymns and return to the church after marching to the jail. The marchers were met at the Post Office by police, sheriff's deputies, and Alabama State Troopers.

At this point the street lights went out abruptly. Some believe the police shot out the lights.

In this version the police started attacking the marchers, chasing some of them into Mack's Café, behind the church. Here the elderly Cager Lee was beat, as well as his daughter, Viola Jackson, and his grandson, Jimmie Lee Jackson. When Jimmie Lee tried to protect his mother, he was shot by Trooper Fowler.

But, this is not the only version of what happened that evening. In another version, the marchers were not just planning to march peaceably to the jail and back, they were planning to break out Mr. Orange.

Planted near the church were broken bottles and bricks, that the marchers used to knock out the street lights and then to attack the law enforcement officers.

At this point the troopers used their batons to protect themselves from the marchers who had transformed into rioters before their eyes.

When two troopers, Fowler and Higginbotham, were sent into Mack's Café, they were both attacked. Inside the Café, Higginbotham went down after being hit in the head by a brick or a bottle.

At about the same time, Jimmie Lee Jackson attacked Trooper Fowler and attempted to take his gun. At this point, Fowler shot Jackson in self-defense. (Coleman Keane, an FBI Agent from Chattanooga, corroborated this version of the story at the time and again when the Grand Jury charged Trooper Fowler with first and second degree murder in 2007.)[3]

---

[3] *Two attempts to try Agent Fowler soon after Jimmie Lee Jackson's death were not successful. In 2010, after the third Grand Jury, Fowler was tried, and pled guilty to manslaughter. He was sentenced to six months in jail, and served four months. Of course, there are some who would have liked to see him spend much longer than that*

Obviously these two stories have very different interpretations of what happened that evening. Many of the key people involved in the incident that night are no longer alive, and many of the medical and other records from that evening have somehow been lost.

---

behind bars, and some who thought any amount of jail time was wrong.

Additionally, one way or another (again the details vary according to who is telling the story), the press cameras that were present that evening were ruined, and no pictures from that night seem to have survived either.

But regardless of what happened leading up to his injury, Jimmie Lee Jackson was hospitalized with his wound, and died eight days later in a hospital in Selma; more than 8,000 mourners attended his funeral.

Considering Jackson a martyr, Pastor Bevel suggested a march to Montgomery to protest Jackson's murder. On March 7, six hundred marchers left Selma headed towards Montgomery.

The "Bloody Sunday" march ended abruptly at the Edmund Pettus Bridge when the marchers were attacked by state troopers with whips, nightsticks and tear gas. Fifty marchers were hospitalized. ABC was on-site to record the march, and broadcast the horrific attacks.

Bloody Sunday Violence

Two days later, Dr. King led a second march to the Edmund Pettus Bridge. The marchers halted at the bridge when ordered to stop, rather than repeat the violence of Sunday. Many who had traveled to Selma to participate in the march were disappointed that the march did not continue.

Dr. King assured them that a third attempt would be coming. Three white ministers who had come to the area for the march were beaten with clubs that night. Two days later, Reverend James Reeb, one of the white ministers, died of his injuries.

Governor Wallace flew to Washington, D.C. to discuss the situation with President Johnson. Johnson informed Wallace that National Guardsmen would be expected to protect the marchers the next time.

President Johnson

A week later, Federal Judge Frank Johnson ruled in favor of the marchers, *"The law is clear that the right to petition one's government for the redress of grievances may be exercised in large groups...and these rights may be exercised by marching, even along public highways."*

Johnson also ordered Wallace not to interfere with the marchers. More than 3,000 marchers left Selma to start the fifty-four mile trek. Marchers averaged twelve miles a day, camping by the side of the road each night.

The marchers were protected by the recently federalized Alabama National Guardsmen.

By time they arrived in Montgomery, there were over 25,000 supporters waiting for them. Dr. King spoke to the crowd from the steps of the capitol building,

"Selma, Alabama became a shining moment in the conscience of man. There never was a moment in American history more honorable and more

inspiring than the pilgrimage of clergymen and laymen of every race and faith pouring into Selma to face danger at the side of the embattled Negroes."

A sad footnote to the Selma Marches was the shooting of a white housewife from Detroit who was driving marchers from Montgomery back to Selma when she was shot and killed by KKK members.

After the Selma Marches, President Johnson said of the March, *"At times history and fate meet in a single place to shape a turning point in man's unending search for freedom. So it was at Lexington and Concord. So it was a century ago in Appomattox. And so it was last week in Selma."*

After that President Johnson pressured Congress to pass the Voting Rights Act of 1965,

"It is wrong – dead wrong – to deny any of your fellow Americans the right to vote in this country...Their cause must be our cause, too...Because it's not just Negroes, but it's really all of

us who must overcome the crippling legacy of bigotry and injustice. And we shall overcome."

Within five months Congress had passed and President Johnson had signed the Voting Rights Act. And within three weeks of the signing of the Act, more than 27,000 blacks across Alabama, Louisiana, and Mississippi had registered to vote.

CIVIL RIGHTS IN ALABAMA
BRIEF TIMELINE

1721
The first slaves arrive in Alabama.

1818
Dred Scott lives in Huntsville and Florence, Alabama for twelve years before moving on to St. Louis and then on to free territory.

1828
After gaining her own freedom, Sojourner Truth sues to retrieve her infant son, who has illegally been sold to a man in Alabama.

1876-1965

Jim Crow laws throughout the South mandate segregation.

1881

A school for blacks is started in Tuskegee, Alabama by Booker T. Washington.

1896

George Washington Carver becomes head of the Agricultural Department at the school in Tuskegee.

1900

The first high school in Birmingham, Alabama for black students opens with eight students (more than 18,000 black students graduate by 1959.)

1931
In Scottsboro, Alabama, nine young black men are falsely accused of raping two white women.

1941 – 1945
The Tuskegee Airmen perform amazingly well throughout the war, taking out over 400 enemy planes, and not losing even one of their own.

1946
Booker T. Washington is honored on a U.S. coin.

Supreme Court decision: Segregated interstate bus travel is not constitutional.

1947

Thirteen blacks and whites travel on a bus across the South to test the new Supreme Court ban on segregated bus travel. They are met with violent resistance.

The first of over 50 bombings (in 18 years) earns Birmingham the nickname "Bombingham."

1950

In an example of "separate and not equal," schools in

Alabama average 48 black students/ classroom, while white classrooms average 35. Approximately $60/year is spent on each black student, while an average of $120/year is spent on each white student.

1954

Twelve hundred (1,200) white businessmen meet in Selma, organizing the White Citizens Council to protest school desegregation after the Supreme Court's *Brown versus Board of Education*.

1955

The Supreme Court orders lower courts to use "all deliberate speed" in desegregating schools.

Rosa Parks refuses to give up her bus seat to a white man, and is arrested. In response, the Women's Political Council (WPC) helps Dr. Martin Luther King, Jr. begin the Montgomery Bus Boycott.

Dr. King is president of the new organization, the Montgomery Improvement Association.

1956

The first black student is admitted to the University of Alabama. When the white students riot, Autherine Lucy is suspended. When the NAACP pressured the University, they expelled her instead.

(In 1988 the University readmitted her, and in 1992, Autherine Lucy Foster graduated from the University with a masters, along with her daughter, Grazia Foster, who graduated with her bachelors.)

Nat King Cole is attacked by six white supremists in Birmingham when performing with an integrated band.

In the *Southern Manifesto*, Southern congressmen call for resistance to the Supreme Court-ordered desegregation caused by the Brown decision.

The buses in Montgomery, Alabama are desegregated after more than a year of boycotts.

When the NAACP is banned in Alabama, Reverend Shuttlesworth helps organize the Alabama Christian Movement for Human Rights (ACMHR) in its place.

The Alabama State Legislature asks Congress for money to relocate blacks from Alabama cities to Northern/Midwest cities.

1957

In Tuskegee, blacks boycott local businesses to fight city redistricting. (Two and a half years later the U.S. Supreme Court rules that the boundary-altering law is unconstitutional.)

The homes of black leaders and several black churches are bombed in Montgomery.

In response to court orders to desegregate the schools, Reverend Shuttlesworth tries to enroll his children at Phillip High School – he is beat by a mob.

1958

Reverend Shuttlesworth spearheads a bus boycott in Birmingham. (The Federal court mandates desegregation the following year.)

1960

Six years after the Supreme Court has ordered them changed the schools in Alabama remain segregated.

Rev. Martin Luther King, Jr. is arrested and jailed on yet another trumped up charge – this time it is for driving in Alabama with a Georgia license. (It is one of twenty times he will be jailed.)

Rev. Shuttlesworth's children are arrested while riding a Greyhound – the charge is violating school segregation laws.

1961

In response to new federal laws prohibiting segregation on interstate transportation, Freedom Rides begin between Washington D.C. and New Orleans, leading to many attacks in Alabama.

City officials in Birmingham, Alabama vote to close public parks, playgrounds, and golf courses, rather than integrate them.

1963

At his inaugural address, Alabama governor George Wallace promises "segregation now, segregation tomorrow, segregation forever."

Rev. Martin Luther King, Jr. and other ministers are arrested during a protest march in Birmingham, in "Project C." While locked up, Dr. King writes his famous *"Letter from a Birmingham Jail."*

When hundreds of black children in Birmingham, who are preparing for another protest march, are attacked by police (with dogs) and firefighters (with hoses), the national outrage is tremendous.

Two black students enroll at the University of Alabama. Governor Wallace, acting as University registrar, blocks the students from entering the school to register.

The Sixteenth Street Baptist Church in Birmingham is bombed; four young black girls are killed, again bringing a national outcry.

Every white high schooler in Tuskegee's High School withdraws from the school when five black students enroll.

1965

Jimmie Lee Jackson is killed in Selma, Alabama during a protest against voting rights violations.

Reverend King leads three marches across Alabama from Selma towards Montgomery in protest of the voting rights violations.

The Voting Rights Act of 1965 is signed by President Johnson. In the first nineteen days after its passage, more than 27,000 blacks register to vote in three Southern states.

1967

Alabama is ordered to desegregate its public schools.

1970

Governors in Alabama, Florida, Georgia, and Louisiana vow to fight school desegregation.

1982

Wallace wins his fourth term as governor of Alabama, this time running on a platform of racial and religious tolerance.

CONCLUSION

The non-violent Civil Rights movement was met with significant levels of violence at every level. But throughout it all, men like Reverend Shuttlesworth and Dr. Martin Luther King, Jr. insisted on turning the other cheek, at the same time they continued their fight against injustices.

As we come to the end of our mental flight, we would all do well to remember King's words: *"Injustice anywhere is a threat to justice everywhere."* And *"true peace is not merely the absence of tension; it is the presence of justice."*

We've come a long ways since these troubled days, but the fight is far from over. It is necessary to be ever vigilant even now.

****

This book is far from a complete look at Civil Rights in Alabama, but I hope it has been enough to give you a good look at what has happened in this state in this regards.

ABOUT THE AUTHOR

Catherine Jaime has been teaching for more than thirty years, but she is continually saddened by the lack of history knowledge among adults and students of all ages. Through books like this, she hopes to help bridge some of those gaps, particularly in this important topic – Civil Rights.

More of Catherine's books can be found on her website: www.CatherineJaime.com.